Dav:
Here's some work
often without
rhyme or reason.

There's a Fractal
in My Soup

Cheers!
Jim

Poems by

JAMES C. MACDONALD

 FriesenPress

One Printers Way
Altona, MB R0G 0B0
Canada

www.friesenpress.com

Cover Art by Samantha Meli

ISBN
978-1-03-917616-4 (Hardcover)
978-1-03-917615-7 (Paperback)
978-1-03-917617-1 (eBook)

1. POETRY, CANADIAN

Distributed to the trade by The Ingram Book Company

ALSO BY JAMES C. MACDONALD

PRICKING BALLOONS

For all my superb English teachers, those special people
who inspired me
and taught me the beauty of language,
and
to my buddy, Lubo Mykytiuk,
a fine actor and another lover of poetry
who left us much too soon

Table of Contents

Summer

The heart is mellowed
When love blossoms like a rose
Its thistles subdued

Roots: A Song of Being

What is ancestry, asks the sage,
Just an illusion upon the page,
A past obscured by human time,
Extolled by poets addicted to rhyme?

What alchemy can discover
Our truth and being to recover
Original blood, flesh, and bone
That is truly, eternally, our own.

Ancients thought to preserve their race
By committing to a state of grace,
Flesh into canopic vases
Hoping for union in mystic places.

But all tribes wish to know the truth
Of relationships from babe to youth,
Sapient elders, king, or slave,
Making our family line proud and brave.

Whatever form your ancient lands,
Inhabited farms or roving bands,
Pastoral or desolate moor,
Common spirit utters a cri de coeur.

The names may change by continent,
But aren't we all of the same descent?
Chebe to Chang to Duque to Fife,
The world belongs to ancestral life.

We should know and revere them still,
Very rich or poor for good or ill,
They are deep in us, hawk or dove,
Linked purely by the genesis of love.

Sisyphus Regained

Some say Sisyphus accepts his lot,
A life more complex than a Gordian knot,
Success parried by failure at every turn,
Not an end in sight that he can discern.

Is one born for eternal recurrence,
A mischievous fate needing great endurance,
A punishment for resisting petulant gods,
Hoping mortals can't beat Las Vegas odds?

True courage and rebellion are not in vain,
They're the opposite of being insane,
Sisyphus needs one more push to say
I've had enough, it's a nascent day.

You can't live in an immutable trance,
With that extra roll, you can advance
To the other side of a Megiddo hill,
Infinite hell conquered by human will.

Waiting for Theseus

In a Jungian trance,
She dreams of existence
As a psychic labyrinth, eluding
The monster whose only goal is stealing
Her soul.

She waits in this world hermetic,
A nightmare truly systemic,
For Theseus and his courage
To challenge the monster with rage
And hate.

She identifies what is real or not
With confidence in her nature of thought
To transform circumstance with reasoning
With no weapons or a string, collapsing
The illusory maze.

The fated spell instead
Is broken
By her patient will to awaken
That hidden, deep-seated sense of being
That sends the phantom creature reeling
To myth.

Ariadne on Día

She plays morosely on her
Mini harpsicord,
Abandoned by deception even after
Legendary deeds,
Translating furiously
Tragic memory
And all the fears and doubts of
Bitter loneliness
Into a syncopation
Melding heart and mind,
Music artfully mating the conscious
To the unconscious,
Her abilities harmonizing with the rhythm
Of the universe,
Raging against betrayal and
Specious promises,
Surviving the taunts even of her peers
Those modern sirens,
Jealous of her fortitude and
Her Rhean spirit.

She rebels, seeing a future
Of her own making,
Not the fate of some oracle or
A mischievous god,
And she plays, in celebration,
Vibrations of joy,
The cathartic music of time,
Always her music.

Medusa Wept

Medusa wept for her plight,
Judged too beautiful for happiness
By jealous Athena who, hating competition,
Transformed her mortal rival
Into a monster.

Medusa's hair thickened with slithering serpents,
Her shoulders sprouted wings,
Her body was covered with rock-hard scales,
Her cold eyes turned all creatures
To stone.

Lonely, a reluctant outcast, forced
By a cruel destiny
To be feared by all the ancient world,
She was offered solace only by
Her compassionate
Sisters.

But trident in hand,
Free from knowing humiliation,
Poseidon emerged from the waves,
Immediately seeing Medusa as a marvel,
A sea-kindred spirit.

Unlike the immortals, he saw great qualities:
Security and power in her stare,
Beauty in her deformity,
And relaxed without fear
In her soft, caressing, writhing hair.

No tears could shade her eyes now,
No need to feel alone,
Defying spells while rejoicing,
Two loving souls in compassionate,
Fluid embrace.

The Beguiled

What do we make of this modern world,
Where the disingenuous boast of their stigmata,
Persuaded by political magicians
To profit the greedy utilitarians.

From tragic circumstances not forgotten,
Some leaders offer Platonic shadows,
Generous, illusive personal treasures,
Privileges gained by despotic measures.

Assumptions become proofs, circles now squares,
The unwary deceived, but unlike Thomas,
They can't touch the holy to make judgements,
Fearing truth and loss of entitlements.

They accept a myopic view of history,
The past actively mutating the present,
The thoughtful, with patience, who disagree
Are fixed upon a symbolic Tyburn Tree.

However recent for all those enslaved,
Unless alive to tell their story,
The sins of the fathers should not be an inheritance,
Despite hypocrites wanting compliance.

These dissemblers with parochial guile
Force the innocents to favour blood over wisdom,
But those who reject being beguiled
Must convince opposites to be reconciled.

The Little Kid in the Front Row

1958 at the height of bebop with jazz,
All art developed with pizzaz,
No less by Art Kane's enthusiasm
To create the photo, *A Great Day in Harlem.*

57 musical giants united at 5th and Madison,
Immortalized at the heart of their profession,
Gillespie, Russell, Krupa, and Dickenson,
Williams, Young, Monk, and Golson.

When Basie sat, neighbourhood kids emerged
From nearby flats, and as they all converged,
No one knew that confusion would reign
Like an intricate improv by John Coltrane.

Discordant cries vibrated throughout,
But Kane orchestrated this chaotic bout,
Setting the boys in their front row places,
An arpeggio of bewildered faces.

One little kid and maybe more,
Sensed something approaching musical lore,
A feeling of strength to be in the presence
Of soulful genius at its transcendent essence.

The Accident

He hit the dog and cried
And had a hard time
Recovering,
Even days after it died.

The car for transportation
Seemed now a warlike thing,
A weapon,
A device for senseless destruction.

He sat in his car seat now lonely,
Doing crossword puzzles
To assuage the guilt,
However unearned in his fragility.

Despite how carefully he kept on track,
He felt marooned in his mind,
Losing his innocence
In a moment he could never get back.

The Anatomy of Perfection

What is perfection and does it even exist
When much of life
Is like a splinter in the foot,
Annoying but livable?

Or even when major trauma
Seeks to expose our limitations,
Can't we just exist
With the impossible?

Some say that striving for and naming perfection,
When not pathological,
Makes the imperfect, perfect,
Creating a language of hope and comfort.

Don Larsen's perfect game, golf's hole in one,
Math's zero, absolute zero,
Perfect verb tense, perfect pitch,
All forms of the numinous—a butterfly.

All wonders for sure, mimicking perfection,
Satisfying laity and expert,
Closing the gap created by sullen philosophers
Like the sad weeper, Heraclitus.

Every response seems inadequate,
But one category supersedes all others,
Something that defines us, something simple,
Something social, something individual.

Something in the spirited Rabelais,
And in Sterne and Swift and Sharpe,
And Ball and Chaplin and Williams,
The ultimate human perfection—
Laughter!

Aristotle's Curse

If only good ideas could mature
Like fine wines,
Continuous rational connections preferred
To fuzzy dictums and didactic signs
With a purpose to expose,
Using a clear mind and a valid premise,
The barbarians and the oppressive elite
Who manipulate Aristotle's logic,
Not for freedom, but for power and control,
Reducing the populace to conformists,
The majority like anesthetized Prufrocks,
Submissive, fearful, and disaffected,
Broken souls who must reconnect
To end this irrational political mysticism
With classical wisdom and thought,
Recommitting to the elegance of a perfect syllogism.

Out of the Shadows

Will you come out of the shadows,
So I can see your walk and your smile again?
It's been so desperately long.
Will I recognize you?

If I can see your walk and smile again,
Despite how you have aged,
Maybe I will recognize you,
And this new reality can become a memory.

Despite how you have aged,
You are probably still graceful.
This memory can become a reality,
Even happier than in times before.

You were always so graceful
When you walked with a gentle air,
With a happy step like in times before,
Exposing your charming smile and fiery eyes.

Your walk with a gentle air
Will be a clue to your identity,
Along with your fiery eyes and charming smile.
Will you please come out of the shadows?

Rainbow Delight

Air and cloud reflections,
Dramatizing an arc of purity
With rare, patterned dispersions
Exposing colourful delicacy.

A gracious, welcoming sky
With a palette for all seasons
Suggests the reason why
We discern prismatic perceptions.

Sun and friendly mist
Create this natural vision,
And when they persist,
We delight in rainbow perfection.

The Persistence of Love

The sun remained although weakened by time,
As we welcomed summer skies before dark,
When the free wind was gentle and sublime,
Moving flowers and inspiring the lark.

Flora and song suffused that dreamlike day,
Sustained us in warmth before frozen nights,
A calm moment to embrace nature's way,
Transcendent even for two acolytes.

This reminiscence we must celebrate,
A feeling a true poet might compose,
For perfection in love's transient state,
As the eternal budding of a rose.

Fall

When branches are bare
We seek an anxious comfort
Knowing darkness comes

The Saddest Person in the World

She sits in the dark as usual,
Staring at mementos while in her favourite chair,
She seems most unnatural and fragile,
An enigmatic, solitary figure there.

She would look up sometimes in distress,
A brief smile to her dear "Petey" bird,
A creature constrained like its mistress,
Rarely a song of delight to be heard.

It wasn't always so, of course,
She had been a vibrant soul,
But circumstance led to remorse,
A shocking, radical change of role.

She could no longer be maternal,
She would feel inner strife,
Her son gone to death eternal,
A soldier in the prime of life.

A child, I sat in the curtained room,
Playing with my mechanical toy,
My mother near, subdued in the gloom,
I, just a reproach as a living boy.

They talked the past in muted tones,
A sadness that lacked a future,
Memories combined with moans,
Hearts broken; reality hard to endure.

Later, that music of suffering was played again,
Another innocent boy with life so brief,
Another mother sick with pain,
Her world also heavy with grief.

Must a mother like Annie, so compassionate,
Find peace only from that brutal bowing
To that unsparing, wearying force ultimate,
To that ancient cloud of unknowing?

How long must death take a hold,
For spirit and love to be diminished,
To live an existence forever cold,
All feelings deeply repressed or finished?

Was this a life of reminiscence,
Precious thoughts that could be willed,
Or an existential, estranging penitence,
A longing that could never be fulfilled?

The Black Bird (after *The Maltese Falcon*)

No matter how wondrous or profitable,
The quest for the tangible in the mythic
Creates contradictory meditations
On innocence, naivety, and duty,
Vying with the deadly and the delusional.
Then all forms of thought induced by fantasy
Become psychological paradoxes
Leaving true morality ambiguous.

No jeweled bird exists, just imagination,
Making it easier for clever scoundrels
That scour the earth for those dubious fakes
To deceive good people who have sincere hope
That their Black Falcon is the genuine one,
Because they believed other falsifiers
Who caused true harm to various innocents
Who mistook illusions for reality.

Education

Two plus two equals four,
And it shall be forever more,
While Newton with gravity and force
Altered history's course,
So Einstein could further knowledge
With foresight on the edge
To explore reality with evidence,
Higher education based on science,
Ensuring the factual will last,
For generally in the past,
Serious scholars in their teaching
Rarely stooped to indulgent preaching,
But modern demagogues relish ideology,
Opinions, not facts, the new pedagogy:
Instead of an objective need to know,
They just flip the cards of the specious Tarot.

When Time Stops

You're not real, are you?
Not when you're truly gone,
You are everyone
Who watches as you watch,
Silent, from your framed throne
On my dresser.

You're not real anyway
Because real is coffined,
Sincere Anubis craft,
By those professionals
Who lovingly create
Memory art.

You are all whom I knew,
Buried in memory,
So how do we bear loss
Or even separation?
An image provides pause
In art and in life, but,
You're still not real, are you?
Not anymore.

Ten Ways of Killing Time (after Wallace Stevens)

A teacher in Grade Five
Wanted us to stand
And sing dumb songs
About life we didn't know,
So we looked out the windows.

Some wonderful parents
Let us do anything we wanted,
So, even while throwing rocks at trees,
We developed.

Brothers and sisters
Often lived separate, active lives,
But we dreamed in silence together.

We played games
And broke the rules,
Evading boredom
Even though we often suffered.

Some prefer athletic movement,
But contemplating static poetry
Can move us unlike sport.

We read and study just for some connection
To knowledge,
Like drama imitating reality,
Until we leave the theatre.

Traveling is unlike any profession,
A cultural excursion into the unknown,
A way of escape,
Like suicide.

Drifting to the store, languid,
Not driving as usual,
My choice today.

Putting words to paper,
Not with a computer, but with a pen
Seems to prove relativity.

While just sitting,
Suspended in thought,
The whole of existence
Stops.

The Crowd

The crowd sniffs, awaiting a miracle,
Like cold vapours of the Delphic Oracle,
Their favourite poised regally above them,
Spitting out a righteous stratagem.

Despite references so oblique,
And bromides rarely unique,
They respond as usual apoplectic,
Gleeful conformity but anoetic.

Comfortable as Hoffer's true believers,
Unable to recognize mystic deceivers,
They can compress history into a phrase,
And worship with insistent, thoughtless praise.

Feeling generous and never critical,
When stunned by their leader's fall,
And unmoved by the political melodrama,
They just elect another messiah.

Solipsism

In this age of selfies universal,
Does mere indulgence lead to indifference?
Can self-consciousness have no reversal?

Can't one be alone with a modest thought
That doesn't require a mob to see?
What trouble this aberrant mode has wrought,
We've almost forgotten just how to be.

We see ourselves through a camera lens
Until habit makes background meaningless,
And little we care to acknowledge friends,
Our separate souls are all we possess.

It starts innocently for connection,
All life seen through a colourful prism,
But self-obsession shapes false perception,
And the weak self descends to solipsism.

Just Another Day

Just another day, another experience,
Success competing with failure,
Minor victories or minor defeats,
Conditions of life,
But failure though is harder to accept,
So, we often store it in dark recesses
Of the mind,
Like a squirrel's nuts
In a camouflage of trees,
Confusing intruders,
Hoping to avoid an effusion of pain
Exploding into consciousness,
Corrupting clear thought,
But accepting failure as normal,
As normal as success,
Often nourishes the soul,
Making it just another experience,
Just another day.

Pale Horse

Only a memory of normal life,
Like images frozen on a postcard,
The old abandoned in the midst of strife,
These new lepers, not ready for discard.

A pandemic punishes the frail,
Confounding those without experience,
Obeisance to power may now prevail,
Enshrining by decree forced abstinence.

Is the world now a Böcklin Island,
A world of suspended animation,
With modern alchemists who now demand
Conformity, lest annihilation?

Can one live in constant, psychic despair
With few daring souls to assuage the dread,
Schrodinger's cat in its hermetic lair,
Feeling neither fully alive nor dead?

Can reason, not belief, lift the veil
To show that spirit in a human face,
A strength of resolve that will not fail,
Defeating the virus, leaving no trace.

We can't sacrifice or mourn forever,
Flaunting black armbands for those who will pass,
Or shelter those from a life's endeavour,
Falling into a somnolent morass.

Devastating plagues will always exist,
But we must keep fear to a minimum;
Let true science and common sense persist,
Freedom, not Milton's pandemonium.

The Mistral Down the Baume

The Mistral howls like a stricken wolf,
I heard it coming from mountains away,
Carving its sinuous path through vulnerable valleys,
Ripping up natural life better left dormant.

The Baume foams, the hills tremble,
We batten windows and doors to survive,
Everything is moored to resist the blasts,
Shrieking animals secured in barns and basements.

Three, six, or nine days, what will it be?
What destruction will it leave behind?
Roof tiles flung miles from home,
Cars overturned and trees uprooted.

No one is safe before the violence ends,
And this isolation seems never ending,
And tenuous security gives way to fear,
And no obvious respite can lead to madness.

In these days, the earth seems haunted,
At mercy to the whims of nature,
Uncertainty inside, more uncertainty outside,
Like leaving the womb for the tempest of life.

Ode to the Tour de Brison
(For Jack Pical, Robert Brugere, and friends in Sanilhac)

The Tower watches over Vivarais,
Alert to fires seen from its parapet,
History lost after intense attack,
Rebuilt lofty for practical use today,
Guarding Versas Castle and Plan la Tour,
Ancient Joyeuse, Vernon, and Sanilhac.

Legend more congenial to poets,
Jealous Sire de Brison lacking foresight
Recruits Lucifer to save his marriage,
Rejecting the Lord for the devil's threats,
But conscience reconciles the Lord and knight,
The devil betrayed responds in a rage.

He comes every year, same time, same day
To steal one stone from the Brison Tower,
The last stone gone means the end of the world,
But firm, bold will reverses evil's way,
Not crusaders, but builders with power
Make the structure no longer in peril.

Force wasn't needed to create disorder,
With religious wars, slaughter, and neglect,
The Tower's origins remained in mist,
Until visionaries got together,
Locals now with just forests to protect
Still wanted this Cévennes jewel to exist.

The world didn't end with devilish, foul play,
But the epic enhances the story,
With courage shown in both myth and the real,
The Tower of Brison remains today
A constant beacon of hope and glory,
Enchanting in its sweeping appeal.

The Arts

When you are alone

Creating alternate worlds

All is nostalgia

Bruegel's Eye

Perched on the gallows,
The magpie watches over its worldly domain,
The woods, a watermill, a castle, a town,
Bruegel's village dancers,
Gyrating disdainfully in the meadows,
Mocking death,
Like the other magpie
Lounging by an exfoliated skull,
All awaiting another dancer
Swinging on that man-made bough,
The ardent gaze of an artist
Again denying comfort.

A Return to Raffles

The journey was tiring and arduous,
But a pilgrimage is a pilgrimage,
Easier than walking up Parnassus,
Not a whim but recollecting an age.

I hurry to the long bar in suspense,
Hoping to see crossing that sawdust floor
A tiger in all its magnificence,
Although I know it's now lost in folklore.

Kipling and Maugham made Raffles a legend,
And I dream of them sitting there like kings
Greeting the lovers of stories they penned,
Drinking with delight their Singapore slings.

Sadly, in time, reality intrudes,
And my brief, romantic visit concludes.

Translated By—

Is that book or painting truth?
Or is it beauty?
Another question,
Another answer,
Just ask John Keats.

When we speak of truth
Can it be translated literally
Into foreign tongues,
Assuring the sharing
Of common experience?

Does Dostoevsky
Read well in Pashto?
Is his meaning exact for all?
Or is it as deceptive
As Bernini's Daphne?

Artists create
Alternate worlds
In words and in paint
In an allusive vocabulary
Called imagination.

In whatever language or culture,
We can understand art,
Whether obscure or lucid,
Substantially being rooted
In historical derivations.

Writing or painting is never
Perfect transmission
Of thoughts and feelings,
But what is lost in translation
Is often gained on reflection.

People revel in diverse forms
Of communication,
Feeling joy in the sense and in the ambiguity
Of the cryptic Nostradamus,
Of the wizard James Joyce,
And of the mysterious Dead Sea Scrolls.

The Paris Café

Another day in a Paris café,
Artists scuttling by on Rue Mont Thabor,
Native, or alien, or émigré,
Curious faces I cannot ignore.

You can tell my writer friend by his eyes,
Lidded, bloodshot, and forever darting,
Rejected again but not a surprise,
Still focused on words of his own making.

The old draughtsman passes all stained with paint,
Always creating with heart and with skill,
Dull critics dismissing his art as quaint,
Although he has talent within him still.

The musician whistles a charming tune,
But she can't escape the ingrained habit
Auditioning every afternoon,
Hoping her fans will understand her wit.

That dancer is ready to entertain,
Floating effortlessly across the way,
Always hiding his deep muscular pain
That exists from morn to the end of day.

That actor walks tall, but hiding her face,
Wanting to be known but not to be seen,
Doing everything with style and grace,
A life transfigured by the movie screen.

I know them all seeing their airs and gait,
Their success and failure and pure heartache,
Waving as they pass, I smile at their fate,
As they fulfill their lives all for art's sake.

Artists at Gare Saint-Lazare

Looking around that old station
In plein air,
Bolts and glass and steam and smoke,
Consecrated by colour on canvas,
Those trains puffing slowly,
Deceptive mimesis of movement,
Translating the once tangible engines
Into shadowy chaos,
Solid now only in sformata impressions,
A trick of mind and sight,
Pigment flowing from those brushes,
Freezing time
To awaken, eternally,
Our buried imaginations.

Those Who Seek Beauty

Those who seek beauty
In those alternate worlds set apart,
With imagination eager for symmetry,
Love the freedom to be lost in art.

The quest is not to fill the void,
A life of loss and misery,
Mental conflicts proposed by Freud,
Awe reduced to therapy.

All the arts are an inheritance
Uniting our senses in harmony,
Even when depicting lives off balance,
They create notes like a joyous symphony.

With contemplation and knowledge,
And the desire to live in delight,
Our perceptions are a human privilege
To experience brilliant, aesthetic insight.

No Mean Tempest

The epicene Ariel
And deformed Caliban,
Invisible and visible polarities,
Both trapped in a rounded sleep,
Revived only when on stage,
Theatrical presences
Subject to the demands
Of a ruling magus,
A puppeteer of human souls,
Who gives only temporary freedom
Between performances
To all who follow his will.

So, all actors, airy or real, on whatever stage,
Should beware of disaffected authority,
Those artists who create illusions
To control dreams and reality,
Like Pied Pipers,
Until rats become children.

Rima: Art and Love in Terza Time

When I am procrastinating,
I retreat into suspension,
Indulging in focused dreaming.

Rima, my double expression,
Rima, all my romantic soul,
Rima, my wordly companion.

My heart and mind must take control,
Two Frostian roads, which to take,
Another curious amphibole?

Is there an anxious choice to make,
Forsaking one for the other
Unconsciously, and then to wake?

A dream is a great restorer,
But we must also use reason,
Joining love and rhyme together.

The Vagaries of Fashion

The origins were practical enough,
Observe the animals and dress in fur,
A peasant's world view of living rough,
For body warmth and movement, not allure.

Soon indulgent elites with their riches
Changed common shapes for showy eminence,
Affectations for princess and princes,
Courtly robes now expressing elegance.

Now fashion, not clothing, became in vogue,
An attempt at individual flair,
Some artists delighting in being rogue,
Non-conformists keeping people aware.

Strange in this new age of identity,
Stronger forces dictate cultural form,
And artists reject singularity,
If special interests decide the norm.

They say fashion is just colonial
When sensitive masters without reason
Use cultures just for the superficial,
Not resisting such artistic treason.

Critics denounce this appropriation,
Compliance the cruel standard for courage,
And ignoring or forgetting tradition,
Do they not see art also as homage?

Confident designers must make a choice,
Using history and culture and magic,
Resisting critics to maintain your voice.
Surrendering conscience will be tragic.

Pas de Deux

He swings her, a fluttering butterfly,
Adagio perfection
Creating a measured movement
En pointe earth to sky
Transcending her own temporal being,
Integrating art of muscle and mind,
Harmony of the Vitruvian kind.

He, by himself, leaps and flies,
A soaring adventurer,
She responds delicate and wise
Exuding a mythic power.

But they reunite restrained,
Eloquent equality,
Joyous completion, sustained
By individuality.

Modern Art

Put a pile of poop
On a New York City stoop
That will be the rage of critics,
But anathema to cynics.

They will call themselves artists,
And rebellious relativists,
Delighting in neurosis and shock,
Not caring if traditionalists mock.

They see the modern as kinetic,
So they create a new aesthetic,
Making all the world their palate
From junk to wraps to Russian roulette.

They ascend to celebrity status
By being deliberately contemptuous,
Deviating from social norms
To sell the rich their most outrageous forms.

These avant-garde love the turmoil,
With op, pop, mixed, and conceptual,
But if you're a skeptic wallowing in their goop,
Don't forget to eat your Campbell's soup.

Winter

Snowy winter skies

Mock the lost, verdant seasons

Chilling memories

The Sacred Tree

Snatch the branch from that Golden Bough,
And kill Diana's old priest,
Reinvigorating Nemi Garden,
Fertilizing the near-barren land
In the eternal struggle
To unite human and divine.

So we kiss under the mistletoe
At this precious time of year,
For both pagan and pious,
Not understanding this innocent sign of love
Was once grave ritual,
Was murder under that Holy Wood.

The Romance of Cemeteries

Wandering through graveyards
Forces us inwards,
Resurrecting the past,
Confronting evolution at last.

What we call ghosts
Are merely mischievous hosts
Conjured by our waking dreams,
As elusive as ever-flowing streams.

We search for truth among these tombs,
But more than truth, it's fear that looms,
Fear that's locked in those vaults,
Physical barriers to our psychic assaults.

No bodies here rise like Lazarus,
Just nightmares felt by all of us
Trying to make sense of life-and-death moments,
Until we meet under those stone-carved monuments.

The Necropolis Express

No death is untimely for the dead,
Just for the living
When they take the Necropolis Express,
London to Brookwood Cemetery
To bury more dead,
Lives that jealous time has ended.

They say rest in peace,
But no one really understands that,
Because, in the future,
Bodies are dug up
Like the embalmed Tut,
Or your next-door neighbour,
By treasure hunters,
By developers,
By archaeologists,
For after the rituals and the rites,
After the plainsong,
The only death that lives is memory.

The only journey that is real
Is that gloomy ride
On the Necropolis Express.

Embalmed Dictators

They hope their secular saints don't decay,
Lenin, Stalin, Mao, Ho, and the Kims,
Turned to clay like the foes they turned to clay,
First, crippling their minds, then crushing their limbs.
Dictators with other cruel martinets,
Ghosts living by the embalmer's magic,
Are staged gods in medicated caskets.

Tamed cults file by seemingly heartsick,
Preserving illusions of common sense,
Preserving the nightmare of rebellion,
Preserving spurious benevolence
For gullible pilgrims' false redemption,
With rulers in formaldehyde glory
Displaying truth expunged from history.

Old Barns

I love old barns,
The more run down, the better,
Always grey, weathered,
Moldy struts framing rotting hay,
Bat friendly with mouse hostels,
Rusting farm machinery
That junk pickers like to restore
Making the real past elusive.

But somewhere hidden deep in their bones,
Even when the sun shone,
And the bales were fresh,
And the beams were strong,
The intimations of corruption existed.

I try to understand these entropic mysteries,
The inevitable neglect, the necrosis of spirit,
Manifested in these skeletal relics.

Throwing Tablets Down a Well

Is there any preparation for death,
A rational, foolproof anodyne
That satisfies even the most cynical,
Or is it total fear of corruption?

The poet feels the anguish,
And posits dark clouds,
And the pain of disintegrating bones,
And the regret of no eternal waking.

Like those sentient Kerameikos Greeks,
Throw your tablets down that well,
Curse your enemies and that infinite nothingness,
And put a dog's head on your tomb.

Archaeology

Such curious professionals
Probing earth for precious objects,
Scattered by aboriginals
Who often knew what time protects.

From Ur to ancient Babylon,
From dry Egypt to Sutton Hoo,
They find mummies filled with natron
And rare sculptures of ormolu.

Ancient lives are resurrected,
And languages semiotic,
The Rosetta stone collated
Aged hieroglyphs and demotic.

Mature cultures in antique lands,
Once under dense forest and dust,
Formidable Angkor still stands,
And Pompeii's site has lost its crust.

Decorating Lascaux aven,
Heightened glow of animal life,
Images profoundly graven,
Ice Age art modelled with a knife.

From Stonehenge to Easter Island,
To Mary Leakey's fossil quest,
Traces of humankind will stand
As treasures of great minds obsessed.

But detectives of existence,
Even with their dogged success
Can't unearth that hidden presence,
That mystery of consciousness.

The Puzzle of Zoology

Do zoologic creatures see their future?
Is that knowledge part of their culture?
Or do they exist without that insight,
Ruled instead by the daughters of the night,
Those spirit Fates who prefer illusion,
Laughing while creating confusion.

Do these natural creatures remember,
However brief and however obscure,
Familiar people, obstacles, and other beings
Like birds flying or bees buzzing,
Or is it just mechanistic behaviour
That governs those conscious but unaware?

Sea mammals, fish, and ruminants,
The smallest bugs to the biggest elephants
Inspire science and religion to speculate
On the nature of being ultimate,
But be it Saint Francis, Audubon, or Goodall,
The secret of all life continues to elude them all.

What Can Escape a Black Hole?

Toss a ball of light
Into a black hole,
And miss it forever,
Lost in gravity,
Unlike an idea
Penetrating a brain
And disappearing
With no body or weight,
Until a reaction,
Ineffable, not chemical,
Bounces around inside a skull,
And floats back out
Through eyes, ears, and mouth
With the speed of enlightenment,
Surprising the physicists
Who can't measure thought.

Kafka's Dream

Was Pavlov's dog happy?
Slobbering for its treats,
Its will anesthetized,
Its behaviour ruled by
The cruelty of
A tinkling bell?

Are we humans the same?
Nothing but clumsy tools
Twisted by fate
Into automatic golems
Of self-abnegation,
Of crippling self-hatred.

Can the natural self
Become predictable,
Controlled by clinicians
Handing out certainty
Like Halloween candies
To the susceptible?

Or is real happiness
Personal rebellion,
Not conditioned response
To everyday contingencies,
Not comfort and safety,
But the danger of choice?

There's a Fractal in My Soup

Without autonomy
The mind wearies and then atrophies,
So instead, choose,
Like the brave Wallendas,
To slide along life's tightrope
Or end up like Gregor Samsa.

Laff in the Dark

You take Laff in the Dark,
The spooky carnival ride,
Out of planned excitement and fear,
Phantoms and skeletons
Suddenly popping out of sinister walls,
Ghostly sounds echoing in your mind,
Mirrors distorting your fragile identity,
So you can hold your partner
And scream without shame,
Pretending excitement and fear
To escape the mundane world
For a momentary thrill
That you can control,
Until you are back in the sunlight
Where most real emotions return,
When comforting day starts to recede,
When your resistance lowers,
And something deeper in your soul,
Something dreamt in the truth of the night,
When you enter twilight sleep,
Something rare but familiar looms,
Something cold but atavistic.
Can you laugh in the dark?

The Pope's Cadaver

Vile Pope Formosus stood trial,
Although stone-dead for seven months,
Exhumed in his robes and rotted glory,
No hope of imitating Lazarus.

What iniquity requires correction so grave,
Enough to recreate the past,
Treating it as present material,
Especially in its most corruptible form?

Politically ambitious Stephen VI
Ascends by punishing a gross cadaver,
Cutting off three fingers from the blessing hand,
Thus, nullifying history with a blade.

A trial ignited by revenge,
Fancies now revealed as facts,
Truth disguised as blasphemous acts,
Deception supplanting knowledge.

Barbarism by the powerful
Is not endemic to Rome
As it flourishes like an uninvited guest,
And when November comes,
We burn Guy Fawkes again.

The Hush of Snowfall

Falling gently,
Crystalline, brilliant,
Individual flakes of snow,
No two the same,
Each a visual miracle
Land without a sound,
Not cold enough for dissonant crunch,
Piled like fluffy cotton candy
On fields and towns,
A world lost in serenity,
Nature creating a peace
That defies definition.

Remembrance Day

What to make of the delicate masses
Who haven't felt war, except in the news,
Death never haunting us like those maimed souls
Mired, fetus-like in the dank trenches
And the bloody, septic foxholes
Of Ypres, the Bulge, Khe Sanh, or Kyiv.

We see violence in edited spurts,
We see the surface carnage and the futility,
We see everywhere, every day,
The world in disorder on a passive screen,
Feelings distanced by hollow voices,
Witnesses without pain or gore.

We hope the horror of ubiquitous conflict
Will be remembered and assuaged
By the rites, the bugles, and the poppies,
But reading the Apocalypse in silence,
Seeing a Jackson painting of an air attack,
Or seeing slides of Passchendaele
Do not replicate a deafening barrage,
Inhaling real mustard gas,
Or spilling guts in a human abattoir.

Spring

New butterflies blush

In sympathy with the trees

Boasting spring colours

There's a Fractal in My Soup

I looked at my bowl of tomato soup,
Too hot, not ready even to sip it,
Bubbling in the middle and around the edges,
Appearing as a microcosm of chaos,
Like waves from a rock thrown into a pond,
Seemingly without patterns.

It must be those seductive intellectual laws
Forcing my greedy anticipation
Of the pleasures of aroma and taste
To focus instead on a mental irregularity,
A visually eroded seacoast
Being bumped by this soupy turbulence.

Even when I scoop up this precious liquid,
My mouth alive, my palate tickled,
I see the same surface again,
Repeating itself, until digested,
Never ending ripples to a vanishing point,
Savoury existence now in a mysterious, arbitrary flow.

However, if there's a moral to these observations
When you seek profundity in the mundane,
When your mind conflicts with your mouth,
Let the creamy potion caress your tongue,
And don't let quantum mechanics
Spoil your lunch.

Grandma

She came slowly, rigidly, down the stairs,
Delicately holding on to her cane,
Ninety-two years old, deserving respect,
Elegant in her dark, Tunkard attire,
With quaint white lace around her wrinkled neck
And a radiant smile of achievement,
From the effort in getting from her bed
To perform habitual ablutions
As a labour of will, a source of pride.
Then a bright light shone on her pure white hair,
Revealing an unnatural colour,
A redness on the surface of her scalp,
And as we wondered about her new glow,
She cheerily told us how good it felt
From that wondrous stuff in the blue bottle.
Startled, we laughed a little nervously,
Knowing it was Clorox bleach, not shampoo,
Old age playing subtle tricks with her mind,
But those mental regions, though, were still human,
So who could deny joy in one
So close to eternity.

A Mother's Long Road Home

At one hundred, your long day was nearly done,
But lingering thoughts of a rueful death
Were past, so you lived well in the present,
Lucid, spirited, and in unison
With the world and your identity,
For serious thoughts of infinity
Are reserved for those cold, contingent years
When dying young was promise unfulfilled,
And dying old was touched with some regret,
You remained calm, dismissing your old fears,
You were conscious only of precious being,
And that was your answer to everything.

That Cryptic Smile

Outrageous crimes of force beneath the stars
Should be exposed,
Moments of unwarranted rage
Should be forgiven,
Expressions of joy in a joyless life
Should be shared,
Personal and political struggles
Shouldn't crush the spirit,
Confessions that shatter the soul
Should be expressed.

Persephone cries in horror,
But survives death to restore spring,
Beauty in a formless landscape
Elevates Munch's lurid Scream,
Hugo's rictal, disfigured child ·
Laughs forever in defiance,
Tchaikovsky's discordant demons
Couldn't suppress his sweet harmonies,
And DaVinci's melancholy
Did create that cryptic smile.

A Paean to the Femme Fatale

The frustrated lover seeks communion,
A reckless transitory attraction,
An indulgent parody for poets,
Lilith conjured through imagination.

Often, love is not this romantic dream,
It's a reflection of your self-esteem,
You must examine your motivation,
Your prickly vanity in the extreme.

Love is a surfeit of contradiction,
So live some of life without prediction,
Immerse the mind in singularity,
But don't dismiss the power of seduction.

A brief winter heart or poetic pain
Is not an excuse for one to abstain
From that temptress who chills the soul and pen,
But awakens both sacred and profane.

In true connection without myth or rhyme,
A drink spills, hands touch, you forget the time,
An anxious fear enters, you're lost in thought,
You exist in a new world sublime.

But La Belle Dame or triple moon goddess
Can kindle pain, joy, love, and forgiveness
To help overcome total enchantment,
A soul journey finally to wholeness.

The History of Birds

After the rain,
The birds turn out to sing
Of the various possibilities
That soaring and swooping bring
In their glorious panoptic domain
Above the worldly tumult and pain.

Haughty, assertive, and audacious,
They left their clumsy dinosaur forms behind
To laugh at ground-born slithering things,
And the random evolution of humankind,
These now winged marvels of the air
Dance in their realm with balletic flair.

Saved from apocalyptic extinction,
They progressed with beautiful features,
The strength to remain aloft,
And with voice to mock lesser creatures,
But unlike Icarus flying to oblivion,
They revel in the nearness to the sun.

Notre Dame

Floating on the Seine like the bridge of a ship,
Notre Dame commands the Ile de la Cité,
Stained glass, ribbed vaults, and with buttresses flying,
Bold, intimidating, and inspiring.

Grotesque gargoyles, strix, and strange chimeras
Watch aggressively, posing cynically
Over the dull parade of human breath
Slouching towards immunity from death.

Desperate creatures want their salvation
From eight hundred years of terror, strife, and change,
The spiritual within the aesthetic,
The sacred embracing the symbolic.

Bells chime to avert passage
For the apotheosis of the faithful,
Although sometimes failing one like de Molay,
Who was burned in the shadow of the archway.

All that history embedded in the beams,
Recently charred, not like that defamed Templar,
Nothing evil nor transcendent, only chance,
Transfiguring the architects' eloquence.

But human resistance will prevail
By rebuilding anew,
Recreating tradition,
Not reverence for death,
Not memento mori,
But memento vita.

The Flaneur of New Orleans

His walk is deliberate, but not slow,
Enough pace to register impressions,
Enough clear vision to love a tableau,
Sights ever exceeding expectations.

He appears aimless, profoundly detached,
Blessed with a demeanor of confidence,
A curiosity that can't be matched,
One of the crowd despite his affluence.

He's happy at home and always aware,
He never ventures to lurk in shadow,
Observing wistfully without a care,
Never needing to be incognito.

Every day a different sensation,
Enchanting sounds and sights, never static,
This city tossed in wild transformation,
The stage could never be as dramatic.

Tourists flood colourful rues unaware
Of dark forces that condition their lives,
Missing the treasures that stand everywhere,
The old and the new, what dies, what survives.

The flaneur roves the treelined boulevard,
Forsaking all those showing no concern
For ancient masques or the brash avant-garde,
Life in history and in the modern.

There's a Fractal in My Soup

He regards tarot readers without shame
In Jackson Square with fulgent butterflies,
Buskers, painters, and poets wanting fame,
All gathered for the human enterprise.

The flaneur transcends common distinctions,
He's not between worlds as others are,
He looks upon relevant conditions,
Loving anomalies both near and far.

He sees light as in a Vermeer painting,
Smells vines decay in a secret garden,
Hears anguish and joy in children drumming,
Musical caprice in spectral Bourbon.

Tennessee sits at the Carousel bar
As the flaneur passes every day,
With Buddy Bolden playing from afar,
Spirits living for him in their own way.

St. Louis One's vaults are a mystery,
To all but our curious ambulant,
Marie Laveau dwells in his history,
Reminding him that all is resonant.

A connoisseur of life with no Virgil,
A wanderer as artistic hero,
He preserves with an intransigent will,
New Orleans, a noble chiaroscuro.

From Tremé to Quarter to Marigny,
The flaneur is the most adventuresome.
As he roams by the cruel Mississippi,
He embodies almost perfect freedom.

New Orleans Notes

They love sirens like jazz
In this vibrant, wild city,
Vehicles in flight.

A firetruck parades
Apocalyptic Canal,
Dodging the frenzy.

Police cars do wheelies
Over ragged cobblestones,
Taking advantage.

An ambulance pushes
Aside frightened tourists
Who hear but don't look.

Clarion melodies
Bring voodoo spells to subdue
Life and death horror.

But natives know the sound
Of this music night and day,
Such comforting tones.

The Origin of Intelligent Life

Was geology just yawning,
Or were the Klerksdorp spheres,
Seemingly inexplicable artifacts,
Almost perfect discs,
Manufactured by inexplicable hands,
Their motives obscure,
Proving that human intelligence,
Those special ancient beings
Could produce
Curling rocks,
In South Africa,
A mere billion years ago.

On the Other Side of the Street

Each day I walk this side, as others do,
Mostly the same route, really don't know why,
Perhaps easier to round the corner,
As crossing here entails a more conscious choice,
Not a metaphysical crux, of course,
Nothing serious, no "road not taken,"
Passively avoiding those streetcar tracks,
It's morning after all, no coffee yet.

But as I look across the way I see
The static, kaleidoscopic buildings,
Pet stores, a dive bar, a walkup, a church,
A po'boy shop, Crescent City bookstore,
Easy to spot from where I am walking,
A familiar but different world,
Barely noticing the sights close to me
With people pushing by as just shadows.

The other side seems more intelligible,
Viewed from here, on the face of it, at least,
A whole panorama forming a street,
A street with secrets camouflaged with signs,
The depths impenetrable from this side,
Distance being the key to my fantasies.
The key to test faulty human vision,
The key to doors of possibility.

Rarely, I walk back on the other side,
Reluctant to pass the disabled man,
Careful of the risky streetcar rails,
Shadows now here, the mystery now there,
Still, I should cross this threshold more often,
Curiosity should overcome fear,
A change in view, not a revelation,
The clear delight of altered perception.

A Simple Thing

My mind was on art on Julia Street,
A slight, annoying drizzle drifting through,
No need for shelter, just a drop of sleet,
Innocent, common enough day I knew.

A little careless, not cautious, I walked,
Glancing at intriguing window displays,
I approached a man who suddenly balked,
Blindly waving his umbrella my way.

Just a simple act, he apologized,
Nearly hitting my eye, an accident,
Shaken a bit, flustered, I realized
A curious lesson this scene had sent.

What if that fierce point had punctured my eye?
What would my everyday life become?
What glorious events would pass me by?
To what compromises would I succumb?

While dwelling on this fleeting occurrence,
A random breach from this too normal strife,
Would I have to change for expedience,
Or just carry on more aware of life?

Acknowledgements

I would like to thank the team at FriesenPress, led by Julianne McCallum who guided me in all phases of the publishing process. As usual, Janine Young's editing was precise and intelligent. Also, a special thanks to Samantha Meli for her amazing cover illustration. Much of my work depends on libraries that provide comprehensive services and a good working atmosphere. These essential places include the Fort Erie Public Library System (including Ridgeway and Stevensville), the UNLV library of Las Vegas, and the wonderful Main Public Library of New Orleans. And, as always, thanks to Shirley and Bill Hawkey for their continued support.

Printed in Canada